Start Your Marketing Agency

A step-by-step guide to launching your own digital marketing agency.

By: Nader Nadernejad

Before you read this book, I'd like to give you free access to my Udemy course. It's closely related to this book and if you find any of the sections confusing, my online course will make it easier for you to understand. Manually type this link to gain access to the course: https://www.udemy.com/startyourmarketingagency/?couponCode=EBOOK10000

Table of Contents

Acknowledgements, 5

Introduction, 7

Naming Your Agency, 11

Registering Your Company, 18

Creating Your Agency Website, 25

My Top Five Website Design Tips, 28

Five Common Website Design Flaws, 31

Learning About Digital Marketing, 35

Getting Your First Client, 39

Pricing Your Services, 44

Creating Legal Contracts, 50

Purchasing a Mailing Address, 53

Listing Your Business on Google, 57

Phone Skills and Sales Call Techniques, 63

How to Get Inbound Leads, 71

How to Deal with Problems and Conflicts, 79

Errors and Omissions Insurance, 84

Hiring a Virtual Assistant, 87

Your Agency's Next Steps, 93

About the Author, 97

Acknowledgements

I want to thank some important people who made writing this book possible. Though this book isn't a doorstop novel or five decades of PhD research, it combines a significant portion of all my business and marketing knowledge. This has come from hundreds of hours spent toiling away at building my business and working with clients around the world. Though I have much more room to grow and improve, it would be selfish of me not to thank the people who helped me get to where I am today.

I want to thank my girlfriend, Mariah for dealing with my stress and anxiety during the hard times when I was attending school full-time, online teaching, hosting my radio show and working with my clients. You've been a huge support in my life and have done everything you can to make my experience better and my life more enjoyable. Thank you for understanding when I worked for hours on end, most weekends of the year and for supporting me even when things didn't go right. It has been a pleasure to live and grow with you over the years.

I want to thank Sigmund Brower: author, mentor and friend. Thank you for teaching me how to make great videos and tell stories with them. You sparked a passion in me to always do creative work and follow my passions.

I'd also like to thank all my teachers and professors throughout my education who encouraged me to grow. A big thank you goes to Trent Radio in Peterborough and CKDU FM in Halifax for giving me airtime to share my passions. I couldn't have accomplished what I have without the amazing people in my life who have always looked out for me and continue to help me strive to become the best version of myself.

Peace and love,

Nader

Introduction

Welcome to *Start Your Own Digital Marketing Agency*! This book is a step-by-step guide to starting your own digital marketing agency. I've done my best to make this book as simple and easy to read as possible – you won't find any fancy writing or fluff in here. What you will find are concrete tips and tricks about the marketing industry and the information you'll need to start your own digital marketing agency today.

Starting my own digital marketing agency has changed my life. I can't describe how much freedom it has allowed me to create for myself. There's so much business for you out there and I can't wait to show you how abundant it is. Starting and scaling a digital marketing agency is all about having faith in the process. I promise you that you will succeed in the digital marketing space if you are driven and have ambition. Digital marketing will allow you to create a profitable business for yourself, but you need to have the passion and the energy to see it through. Starting a digital marketing agency is an all-or-nothing game. If you want it to support you for years to come, you need to give it your time and energy. Digital marketing agencies are a service-based business, meaning you'll have to invest a lot of upfront time in the beginning stages if you want to see success. I can't stress this enough - *you need to stick through it!*

In this book, you'll learn how to launch your own digital marketing agency from scratch, set up your agency's website, get a legal address for your agency, list your business on Google, get your own number and automated answering system, learn how to pitch your services to new prospects, get your first clients and much more. Toward the end of the book, I'll teach you how to make your agency even more profitable and scale it to compete with the other marketing agencies in your area and around the world. This book will also teach you a lot about the digital marketing space in general. You can also expect to learn about sales, since you'll be the one selling directly to your customers when you get started. A good entrepreneur is a great salesperson.

The chapters in this book are short and get straight to the point. I wanted to make this book that way on purpose to provide as much information as possible. I also wanted to make this book accessible to everyone, so that anybody of any education level can start their own digital marketing agency from the comfort of their own home.

Starting your own digital marketing agency is simple; the hardest part is rising to the top of the industry and getting noticed despite the noise. Another challenge is making your marketing agency sustainable, putting out fires when things go wrong and providing services that are good enough to retain clients. I will teach you exactly how get noticed and run your agency so that you can start your new business armed with the confidence and knowledge you need to be successful. If you have any questions about starting your own digital marketing agency or about this book, please send an email to nader@nadernejad.com with the subject line, "BOOK QUESTION". I try to respond to questions about course content and books within 72 hours. My readers and students always get top priority.

Naming Your Agency

Creating a name for your digital marketing agency is the most exciting part, but it can be frustrating. Everybody wants to pick the perfect name. I know what it feels like, but please don't stress yourself out. I'll guide you through the process and give you some ideas so that you can pick the perfect name for your digital marketing agency.

The first thing most people do when thinking of a new business name is to open a search engine on their internet browser and begin searching all the names they can think of. They do this only to realize that most of their ideas are taken. You need to understand that there are so many great marketing agency names out there. If your name is taken, keep looking. There's an infinite combination of business names and ideas, so please take your time with this step and don't worry about picking the perfect name.

Naming a business requires originality. If you're original enough, you will stand out among the competition. There are many techniques that branding professionals use to come up with business names and I'm going to unveil some of them to you. This could save you hundreds or even thousands of dollars you would otherwise have spent hiring someone to come up with a name. Many people starting a digital marketing agency for the first time don't have the budget to splurge on anything, let alone a business name idea created by a branding expert. I'm going to get into some of the most effective techniques you can use when choosing a name for your new business.

The first rule is to never name a marketing agency after yourself unless you already have a client base or are dying to boost your personal brand image. If you already have clients you work for monthly, they'd probably be willing to support your new business venture no matter what you name it. They already trust you, so it can even help your cause to name your new agency after yourself in some cases. If you don't have a client base, but still want to name the agency after yourself like I did, then you need to be okay with sacrificing your shot at having a more marketable name. Naming your agency after yourself is a personal brand boost. That's why I named my agency Nadernejad Media. Please don't use your name unless you have a good reason to do it. I was willing to make the sacrifice for personal reasons. Ask yourself if you're willing to do the same thing if you're thinking about using your own name.

Let's get into some concrete tips you can use when naming your agency from scratch.

Tip 1: Include customer desire in your business name. One tip you can use when naming your agency is to include the desire of a potential client in your business name. For example, if your target consumers are people who want to go viral in ten days, you could name your agency "VIRALIN10".

Tip 2: Create a name that poses a solution to a problem. Everyone seeking digital marketing services has a problem. For example, one of your clients had been accused – and acquitted – of stealing cheese from the creamery he worked at. He had his name and face published in an online paper, detailing his crime. Every time he applies to get a job at a new creamery, his employers Google him and discover the accusation. Now he can never get a job at a creamery again unless you get rid of his negative Google link. In this case, you could name your agency "Negative Link Cleanup". That name represents the solution to a problem.

Tip 3: Create an agency with a theme. Sometimes it's better to visualize a certain image and brand your agency around it. For example, you could call your agency "Social Fire" and theme your site in a bright orange colour. You could have buttons on your site that reveal animated flames when a customer hovers their cursor over them. This tip works best for creating powerful brand images that people remember. The best part about this is that you don't have to think too hard about what the design will look like after you name the agency. The hard part is actually implementing the design.

Remember to dream big, but also be realistic. Try to be as original as possible, but make sure you can deliver on your promises. For example, if your agency is called "VIRALIN10", then you better make your clients go viral in ten something. Whether that's ten days or ten months is up to you, but you need to deliver on your promises. In the digital marketing industry, it's important to promise big things and deliver even more than what you initially promised. These things are what keeps your clients coming back. You're going to make the most money from your agency because of the clients that keep renewing their contracts with you. You don't want to change clients frequently. Instead, find key clients you can work with and keep them coming back for more business for as long as possible. How long you can keep a client will ultimately determine your success or failure in this industry.

Remember, when choosing a name, you want to keep it short and memorable. Ultimately, it's not about having the best name in the world. It's about the work you do and the exposure you get that's going to determine whether your agency is successful or not. Starting a successful digital marketing agency comes down to your ability to execute your decisions. Give yourself time to create a name you love, but be sure you're dedicated to it before you start your agency; it's harder to change a name once you've created it and published your site. People will remember your company after they do business with you, so you want to make sure you don't have to change your business name when you should be thinking about growing your business instead. This could mean starting from scratch a second time, and you want to avoid having to do that. Your focus should be on doing everything you can to get ahead of your competition, break out of obscurity and impress your clients. If you're naming your marketing agency and want to run the name by someone, try a few family members or friends. At the end of the day, you're going to have to make the final decision on the name you'll use for your marketing agency, but it never hurts to get some insight from people who care about you and your success. Remember to take everyone's advice with a grain of salt, though. Plenty of people have no idea what they're talking about, so remember to use your common sense.

Feel free to bookmark this page while you think of a name for your digital marketing agency. There's no need to rush through this book. Move onto the next step at your own pace. If you're reading out of pure curiosity or for enjoyment, please continue, but you'll do yourself a service by taking the time to think of a name you love before jumping ahead. When you're passionate about your business name, you'll find it much easier to sell your services to other people. Pick a business name that excites you. When you are excited about your business, you transfer that energy to your prospects, which will result in more long-term success.

Registering Your Company

Let's discuss the legal stuff. If you want to do business with a company name (not your own name), this is called DBA or "doing business as". Some states and provinces require you to file for a fictitious name to do this legally. That means you can't jump in and do business immediately without registering that name with your local government. It does sound like a hassle, but it's not too expensive and it's better to have a legally established name for your marketing agency if you want clients to take you and your business seriously.

Before you read this section, research how to register your business in your province or state. The process varies depending on your location, but I will give you some basic information if you live in North America. If you're still confused, feel free to send me an e-mail or look for online educational content that walks you through how to legally register a business in your province or state.

The first thing you need to know is that there are different business models. In this section you're going to learn how to start a business as a sole proprietor. A sole proprietor is the simplest business model because it's cheaper, there's less paperwork and you are your business. What does that mean? That means you file your business tax as personal income and not as a separate entity. Your income counts as personal income, not business income. If you were to launch a corporation or an LLC, then your business would count as a separate entity. You would have to file taxes separately, the deadlines for taxes are often different and if somebody decides to take legal action against you for the work you did (or didn't do), they would have to sue your business. This is more complex because it involves keeping your business assets separate from your personal income. I don't want to teach you how to launch a corporation when you're just starting out because I'm sure most of you want to launch your business with the least amount of hassle. That's why I'm choosing to go over the simplest route of launching your business as a sole proprietorship. This chapter will provide you with general information, but you'll be required to do your own research. I'll guide you through the process step-by-step.

Step 1: Search online the following key phrase: "Register Sole Proprietor (insert state or province)."

Step 2: Do not click on ads or paid links. These places will charge you extra money to start your business. You want to register your business directly with your local government with no third parties involved in the process.

Step 3: Click on the first federal or municipal government link you see, because you want to register your business directly with your government. If you're having trouble, ask somebody who lives near you who operates their own business in your area.

Step 4: Once you've navigated to your official government's business registration page, follow the on-screen instructions to register as a sole proprietor in your state or province. You may need to conduct a business name search to make sure your business name isn't taken. Many government sites provide this service for a fee. Again, there's no way for me to give you a direct link because this will vary depending on where you're starting your business.

When I started my marketing agency in Canada, I registered as a sole proprietor. I navigated to the Ontario government website, entered my social insurance number (SIN) to verify my identity, registered provincially (valid for 5 years) and paid a fee of approximately $60. Service Ontario immediately emailed me my Master Business License and I was ready to go.

I always recommend registering your business online and doing it yourself. It's usually easy to register your own business once you've put in the research. People get intimidated by the paperwork, when in reality, it's usually only a couple of pages of information you need to complete online. Depending on where you live, you may need to visit a government location and register your business in person. Your registration may be valid for less than five years too. In some places, it's valid for a few years and in others, it's valid for a year or less. Research business registration in your area and ask the experts to gain a complete understanding of the business models and registration methods available to you. Remember to read the information from your local government website, because all the information you need is usually published there.

If you still have no idea how to register a new business name in your area, please don't get frustrated and panic. Nobody likes paperwork and bureaucracy, but you only need to complete this step once. After a while, the process becomes simple and easier for you to understand. If you're struggling, try calling your local government office and asking them your questions about business registration. Pick their brains for a few minutes to fix any misunderstandings you may have. Taking the time to register your business at the beginning will reduce the chance that you'll run into legal problems in the future.

I often get questions about partnerships because people feel safer launching a business with a friend. My advice on partnerships is simple: don't do it until you've worked in the industry alone for a while. Partnerships can be amazing, but every successful entrepreneur I've talked to has had a problem with a partnership at some point in their career. It's better to have full control over your first business so that you understand what it takes to run a business. If you do the sales, taxes, accounting, customer service, marketing and general upkeep of your business, you're going to be more well-rounded and better educated in the field than your competition. You also get the added benefit of following your instincts without having to run it by someone else. Why move away from the nine-to-five lifestyle to start your own marketing agency if you have to report to somebody constantly? Take the plunge and do it yourself. Save partnerships for when you're more experienced and know for sure that the person you're partnering with will bring value to your new business.

I know registering a business can be challenging, so if you're having trouble and need help, send me an e-mail and I'll do my best to simplify the process by answering your questions and helping in any way I can. Good luck registering your business! This is an exciting stage, so enjoy every moment of it and don't let the process scare you.

Creating Your Agency Website

After completing this chapter and publishing your website, you will officially have your own digital marketing agency up and running. You'll be ready to accept new clients just like that. There are so many different options available to you when creating a website. You can use HTML coding knowledge to design a website yourself, you can hire somebody to build you a Wordpress site or you can use a drag-and-drop website builder like Wix, Squarespace and Wordpress.

I'm going to give you my number one choice although many people may disagree with it. I think it's the best choice for beginners because anybody can do it, it takes less time and you can have your site up and running in 24 hours or less. *Make your agency site at Wix.com*

I don't make commission sales from Wix and there are no referral links in this book. I recommend using a Wix site because most of you reading this book are entry level. There's no need to spend thousands of dollars on a developer to make you a Wordpress site you may not even know how to use. I recommend a website builder for any first-timer if you have no coding knowledge. This is the best option for solo entrepreneurs because they need to spend their time on making sales and increasing their income at the beginning stages. Time is valuable and you don't want to spend your time on learning HTML or shelling out thousands of dollars before you even get started.

I recommend Wix above any other website builder for marketing agencies because I have found it to be the most intuitive and customizable drag-and-drop platform. It has phone support, and it lets you drag-and-drop things wherever you desire. Their support team is quick to resolve any bugs or conflicts. If you're a web design expert (I am not), feel free to go ahead and create your marketing agency site on whatever platform you want.

If I started my agency on the Wordpress platform, I would be completely lost. I edit my site on a weekly basis and Wix has provided everything I need, including easy customization whenever I want it. No client has ever asked what platform I use or how I designed my site and it performs well on Google search rankings. I get daily visitors that I convert into paying clients just like any other marketing agency website.

Now that I've told you my secrets, let's talk about tips for designing a marketing agency website, as well as some of the typical web design flaws you should avoid when building your site. If you would like to check out my marketing agency site, you can visit www.nadernejadmedia.com. Please feel free to borrow ideas from my site and use it to gain inspiration, but I'd like you to be as original as possible. Don't copy my website because it won't be true to your personality and your brand. You need to design a website around your clients and your goals, not mine. What works for me may not work for you and vice-versa.

My Top Five Website Design Tips

The end goal of your agency website is not to impress your friends and make your mom proud. You need to build your website focused on converting visitors into paid customers. In this chapter, I'll teach you some of the strategies I implemented to do exactly that.

Tip 1: All of the important information goes at the top of your site. The top of your site is the first thing that visitors see, so you'll want to put your contact information there. If potential clients (prospects) contact you directly, it will be much easier to convert them into paying clients. We'll talk more about that tip later.

Tip 2: Use a simple, easy to read font. Don't get fancy and use strange fonts and colours all over your site. Not only will that confuse your viewers and give them a headache, but it will make your site look unprofessional.

Tip 3: Have a mission statement or a slogan on your site. My marketing agency's slogan is "Unlock your unique potential to dominate the media" meaning anybody can dominate the media in their own unique way – and we help our clients unlock their potential to do that.

Tip 4: Have a list of services on your site. This is extremely important. What services does your agency offer? You need to outline your services and give a brief description of each so that visitors know what you can give them.

Tip 5: Write about your target audience. Your website is an opportunity to help readers feel like you understand their problems, which is why you want to use your website as an opportunity to speak directly to your target audience. Are you targeting small businesses that aren't making enough sales? Are you targeting Fortune 500 companies? Find out who your target audience is and figure out what you can say to entice them to buy from you.

I wanted to keep these tips sweet and simple so that you can reference them while building your marketing agency site. When it comes to building a great site, I recommend referencing other marketing agency sites on the internet and using my five tips to help you out. Feel free to borrow ideas from sites you love, but never steal somebody else's work. Being original in this industry will increase your rate of success if you put in the necessary hard work.

Five Common Website Design Flaws

In website design, the devil is in the details. Here are five common agency website design flaws you should avoid if you want to keep visitors on your site and off your competitor's.

Flaw 1: There's no easy way to find information.

It doesn't matter how much information your website has if it can't be found. A simple sidebar or menu at the top of the homepage that links to all your sites pages will suffice for most businesses. If you have many pages that visitors would need to sift through to find what they're looking for, consider adding a search bar to simplify the search process. Some of the best designed home pages use both devices to allow visitors seeking something specific to find the information they need using the search bar and others who are just browsing can use the menu to learn more about your company.

Flaw 2: You're mixing too many colours or fonts.

Your website should be eye-catching but making it a dazzling rainbow of colours or using a different font in every category will turn away visitors, and thus, potential clients. A good guideline to follow is to limit yourself to three colours or fonts, making sure they don't clash with each other. There are many sites with colour wheels to help you find colours that complement each other, and mixing serif and sans serif fonts can be risky – most people find it easier to read sans serif fonts online, though prefer serif for printed documents. When you have designed the site the way you like, have someone else look at it for a second opinion. After a few hours of web page designing it is easy to convince yourself that Comic Sans looks great, but unless your business is targeted toward something more silly or lighthearted, it probably isn't the best choice.

Flaw 3: There's too much clutter.

It is important to fill your website with information, but don't approach your site design with the same technique used to pack a too-small suitcase. Empty space is important, so use margins and don't feel the need to fill every little corner. There is a fine line between giving your website the feel of an overcrowded party and an empty warehouse, so try different layouts until you find a happy medium between the two. Many web design services have templates that can help with formatting, or you can consider hiring site designers.

Flaw 4: The background music is obnoxious.
Embedded music is a sin of web design. Background music is rarely, if ever, needed. It often confuses most visitors as they try to determine the source of the music, or goes unnoticed by visitors with their speakers muted. If you must use background music, feel free to add easy-to-locate controls so visitors can pause it, but most of the time the music will

simply diminish the efficiency and professionalism of your site.

Flaw 5: You're not getting the message across.

The most important part of a website is its simplicity. If a visitor lands on your homepage and can't quickly figure out what your company does, they will leave. It can be an aesthetically pleasing website, but design does not work if it doesn't clearly promote your brand. If your business name, slogan, and an image on the home page can't get the message across, consider changing at least one of them. The goal of your site is to advertise the services your business provides, so keep it simple.

Learning About Digital Marketing

When I created my Udemy course on starting a marketing agency, I got some great reviews, but a frequent complaint was that I didn't give my students enough tips about marketing strategies. I simply assumed that everybody taking the course already had marketing skills under their belt, or at least a crazy amount of self-confidence about digital marketing in the first place. I assumed wrong, so I quickly updated the course with bonus lectures. You can check those out using the coupon code in the beginning of this book.

Since this book is about starting a marketing agency, I don't want to delve into all the details about digital marketing itself. That would completely change the topic of this book, but I'll explain how you can overcome the learning curve to create comprehensive marketing strategies for you clients and be a professional in this industry. Many people don't understand that you only need to have basic knowledge about marketing to start. Most of your clients will have no idea how to use social media or content marketing, have no clue about what a viral video is and won't know how to grow a social following. With basic knowledge, you can start picking up clients who own smaller businesses, like contractors, small restaurants, HVAC companies and more.

Before you get started, I recommend you spend at least a month learning about digital marketing. Here are the steps I recommend you take to learn enough about digital marketing to get started.

> **Step 1:** Learn what all the terms mean. Learn what social media marketing, search engine optimization, copywriting, viral marketing, public relations, content marketing and guerilla marketing mean. Search for other related terms and learn what they mean.
>
> **Step 2:** Learn how to use Facebook, Twitter, Instagram, YouTube, Pinterest and other social

media platforms. Do you know how to create a Facebook page? Do you know how to write a tweet? Can you create photo content for Instagram in under 5 minutes?

Step 3: Learn how to use basic tools for content marketing. Go to www.canva.com and create graphics for free. Create inspiring Instagram content using Canva and tutorials from the internet.

Step 4: Get through my entire Udemy course. It will teach you the ins and outs of the digital marketing industry and how to create basic Facebook ads you can use to grow your client's social media accounts. Buy other digital marketing courses on Udemy. If you can't afford them, you can find free courses there too.

Step 5: Learn marketing automation. Not everything needs to be posted automatically. Tools like Buffer and Hootsuite will allow you to publish social media posts automatically. All you have to do is schedule them beforehand in one sitting.

These are some basic things I recommend you do before jumping into starting your own digital marketing agency. In fact, I jumped in before I knew how to do anything. You can choose to do that too if you're brave enough. I was put under pressure by my clients to learn. After they paid me, I *had* to figure out how to solve their problems and grow their businesses. You don't even really need to learn all of the things I'm telling you to, but those are the main steps I take if you're a person who likes to be ultra-prepared.

Getting Your First Client

Before we begin to talk about pricing the marketing services you'll offer your clients, we need to adopt a salesperson's mindset. If you want to succeed at any business, you can't be weird when it comes to asking for money. You deserve to ask for money because you're the one who's going to provide value to your client. If you truly believe that the services you're offering are worth it, then you ought to have enough confidence in yourself to ask for money.

I recommend working on your people skills as much as you can. Read everything you can on selling. Watch YouTube videos about sales and marketing. Do everything in your power to stay on top of your industry. Improve your digital marketing skills everyday so you believe you're providing the best service possible to your clients. At the end of the day, the sales business is all about confidence and you'll be the person selling directly to your customers when you launch your own marketing agency.

Now, let's talk about numbers. How much should you price your services? It's impossible to directly answer this question, because the answer is always "sell as high as you can and provide them twice as much value." This means that you should try to charge as much as your client can possibly afford and provide an even larger return on investment. If your client pays you $15,000 a month, you should give them $30,000 worth of value. Whether that comes in the form of direct sales or not doesn't matter, but it's your job to close at the highest number you can and overperform to keep your clients coming back for more.

Before we start thinking about large contracts, though, let's stick with the basics. To get good at sales, you need to believe you can make a sale. That's why I encourage my students to make their first sale of a couple hundred dollars before they focus on the big picture. The way this works is simple. Contact everybody you know and offer them marketing services. Send e-mails to local businesses, post classified ads on Craigslist and Kijiji, ask your mom's work friends, beg your aunt or uncle to purchase your services; just do everything you can to sell digital marketing services to anybody you know. Make sure it's priced over $200 and you get bonus points if you sell your first package to a stranger. Once somebody agrees to purchase your services for a month, have them pay you all of the money upfront. None of this getting paid later business. Get them to hand or transfer you the money in full and begin working for them for the next 30 days. Promise them some form of results. In the marketing industry, we call these promises "deliverables". Will you grow their following by 100? Will you get their website more traffic? It can be less tangible too – are you going to SEO (search engine optimize) their site? Promise them something and deliver on those results within 30 days.

When those 30 days are up, you want to re-approach your new client and give them a progress sheet or a report. This is usually a typed report or a PDF you e-mail them, outlining the positive progress you achieved for their business. Perhaps their website traffic increased by 20%. Maybe you got your client more engagement or more fans. It's always best to follow up with a phone call when doing this so that you can use your enthusiasm to make them feel even better about the progress you achieved. Get excited and be confident. This is crucial if you want to retain the client. Remember, your clients want to believe your work helped their business. Use this call as an opportunity to show them it did.

After a follow-up, you'll find that the client will likely purchase your services for another few months. Technically, this client isn't a permanent client because they haven't signed a contract with you. We'll explore 'retainer clients' later and delve into creating contracts to keep clients paying you for longer periods of time, but for now – celebrate! You scored your first client and that's all that matters. You've convinced yourself of your own ability to sell and provide value. Now you need to do this on a much larger scale. In the next chapter, we'll talk about some dynamic pricing options and some techniques you can use when pricing your services with future clients.

We'll also get into some basic contract law to keep you protected as you work with clients in the future.

Pricing Your Services

The first rule of pricing your services is to never list them on your site. If you list the prices of your services on your site, you'll never be able to be able to justify raising them in the future. You may also lose prospects because big prices could result in sticker shock. Your goal is to get your prospects on the phone or speak to them in person and sell them the service that way. It's more personal and they're more likely to trust you, which will justify the higher price tag.

Another rule that I mentioned in the previous chapter is to always provide more value than you're charging for. Do brilliant work and blow your customers away with how well you work on their projects. Get them real results that keep them coming back for more. The quality of the service you provide will keep your customers coming back and will result in referrals. If you put in the work to make your clients happy, your business will continue to grow.

I know many of you are seeking concrete pricing structures in this chapter, so let's talk some actual figures. My recommendation is to sell packages over $1000 as soon as possible and never go lower. Your starting point should be $1000 / month minimum and you should work your way up from there. I understand it's hard to make $1000 sales if you've never sold anything before. It's especially hard in a service-based industry because people aren't paying for *things*, they're paying for *you*. Begin with sales between $250-1000 in your first couple of months. Once you feel comfortable with selling packages under $1000, you can quickly aim to make sales of $1000 and over and stop accepting low-paying clients.

I have divided pricing your services and scaling your marketing agency into phases. You goal is to transition out of each phase to scale your company and make more monthly income. Remember, each service is priced for a duration of one month. Every month, your clients should pay you again. We'll talk about creating contracts in the next chapter, but for now, let's take a look at the phases.

Phase 1: Your First $250 Sale – Make a sale of $250 or higher to convince yourself that you can sell your services.

Phase 2: Sell Multiple Packages Above $500 – After you've done this, you'll convince yourself that you can make an extra $1000 with your marketing business.

Phase 3: Sell Packages $1000 and Above – When you get to this phase, it's important not to compromise. Stop taking clients that pay you under $1000. This way, if you score five new clients, you'll be making $5000 a month or $60,000 a year.

Phase 4: Ask Clients for Referrals – At this point, you should ask your clients for as many referrals as possible so that you can score more business. You should be aiming to sell your packages for over $1000. During the fourth phase, you should continue prospecting and finding more clients so that you can increase your total revenue. During this stage, you want to try to pass the $100,000 mark with your business. Work as hard as you can to get enough repeat clients to bring in a 6-figure annual income.

Phase 5: High Ticket Sales – Once you reach a 6-figure annual income, you need to change things up a little. You're not going to reach a 7-figure income by taking the exact same steps you did in the beginning. Aim to improve your website's SEO (search engine optimization) and Google ranking, get listed on business directories and tell everybody about your company. Your goal should be to make sales well over $5,000 at this point. You may even want to start ending contracts with some of your lower-paying clients from the start if they still happen to be hanging around. If you have running contracts with them, wait for them to end and sever them politely.

These phases are a general overview on how to price your services and how to gradually start selling at higher prices. My mail goal with this chapter is to get you out of the mindset of thinking that everything has a specific price, which simply isn't true. Pricing is flexible and depends on the services you're offering and the value you provide. Pricing also has a lot to do with your client and what they can afford.

When pricing your services, remember that you want to get to a point where you can comfortably make sales without having to worry about justifying your value to yourself and other people. If you don't believe your services are worth money, you shouldn't be selling them in the first place. Convince yourself of your own value before you go out there and start selling to other people. Selling takes confidence and conviction, so you need to invest in yourself from the beginning. Get good at marketing before you decide to launch your marketing agency. Later in this book, we'll talk more about staying on top of the industry and digital marketing, but for now, let's talk about building contracts to make sure you keep getting paid and stay legally protected.

Creating Legal Contracts

We talked about making smaller sales before having a contract in place, and even that is a little risky. It's important to create a legal agreement in order to keep yourself protected and to hold both you and your client accountable. Luckily, you don't need to hire a lawyer to create your contracts when you're getting started. Lawyers would love to have you believe that you need to hire them, but that's simply not the case anymore.

With today's technology, you can use online tools and templates to generate contracts. Sure, it may not be as efficient as having an in-house lawyer draft your contracts for you, but it will save you several thousand dollars over the course of the year, which is money you can *and should* invest back into your business. Using tools and templates to generate contracts is also much better than having no contract at all. Legalese (or legal jargon) isn't that hard to understand if you do your research and read through the entire contract. You contract is probably only going to be about five pages, which shouldn't take you more than an hour to read through and completely understand. See! No lawyer needed.

When creating your first legal agreement with a new client, I recommend using the online business software "AND CO" (www.and.co). AND CO is a free software you can use to create legal agreements by plugging in your contract price, duration of the contract and manually selecting the terms and clauses you want to include. When using AND CO, you'll be able to export your contract as a PDF and e-mail it to your client for them to sign. You can also choose the monthly option for as long as you want if you want to have your client pay you on a monthly basis. By creating these legal agreements, you'll lock your clients into agreements with you and have a steady guaranteed income over an extended period.

If you don't want to use AND CO, you can conduct a quick internet search for freelancer or contractor legal contract templates and fill in the blanks with the specific details and dates related to your contract. Some services may charge you a fee, but many of them are free and all of them are cheaper than hiring a lawyer.

On that note, if you can afford hiring a lawyer, feel free to do it. You will be more protected if you have a lawyer, but it isn't an option for everybody. My job is to make sure that I make as much information available to you so that you can make your own educated decision about what route you decide to take when creating your first legal agreement. Once you get used to creating contracts and getting paid, your business and making sales will feel much easier for you.

Purchasing a Mailing Address

Most companies have a mailing address, and it's a good idea to have one because it looks more professional to customers and allows you to list your business on Google search. Today, you don't need to have a physical office location to get a company mailing address. All you have to do is purchase a virtual office or legal mailing address online. In this chapter, I'll show you how to do just that.

The best part about purchasing a mailing address for your company is that you don't have to live or work in the actual city of your mailing address and you'll still be able to list your business there. For example, I spend a lot of my year between Peterborough, Ontario and Halifax, Nova Scotia, yet my business is listed near the Toronto Eaton Centre. I haven't been to the Toronto Eaton Centre in half a decade. You're probably wondering how that's possible and why I did such a thing. I wanted to list my business in Toronto although I didn't live there because that's where a lot of the business was. I knew big companies were in Toronto and wasn't daunted by the competition of a big city, so I decided to get a virtual office address, so I could use the mailbox to verify my business on Google. I'd also be able to use a fancy address as my company's legal address, potentially scoring higher-paying prospects.

I simply conducted a Google search of "virtual mailbox in Toronto", which brought up several options. I went with a virtual office on Yonge St. close to the Eaton Centre and purchased a package for about $8 a month. Today, my business ranks in the Top 10 pages on Google search for the keywords "marketing agency in Toronto". That may not be fantastic, but it's much better than being listed in smaller cities like Halifax or Peterborough. This decision has scored me more business, generated more leads and allowed me to run what appeared to my prospects as a large company. The best thing about having a virtual office for your business is that you can repeat this process so that it looks like you have several offices. I can launch a virtual office in New York, London, Australia and so on and take advantage of the Google listings in those locations too.

I've used this tactic with my own business and have implemented it with my clients too, generating phenomenal results. I'm in the process of listing my business in different cities at the moment. In each city, I have a Google listing connected to the same number, which allows me to close deals with new prospects every day. In the next section, we'll talk about listing your business on Google to take advantage of your new legal address.

Remember, everything mentioned in this book is for educational purposes. You can choose to skip some of the steps if you wish, but at your own discretion. If you decide to skip registering your business, for instance, that decision is on you. Even if you don't want to purchase a virtual office because you can't afford it, it doesn't matter. Lots of people don't purchase virtual offices. This knowledge is valuable and if you haven't thought of the ideas I'm mentioning before, you're now more valuable to the marketing industry by simply knowing these new tactics. In the next section, we'll talk about listing your business on Google to reach new clients, get more phone calls and increase the traffic to your website.

In the meantime, I'd like you to think of the legal address you want to use for your business. You may have already decided this when registering your business. Just make sure the address you register has a post-box that you have access to. When we list your business on Google, you'll be mailed a postcard with a verification PIN that you'll use to confirm your listing. Also, if you have any questions or anything in this book becomes confusing, remember to check out my free Udemy course that I listed in the opening of this book. You can also contact me by e-mail.

Listing Your Business on Google

Now that you have a legal mailing address for your business, it's time to talk about listing your marketing agency on Google. I'd also like to use this chapter to talk about some of the benefits associated with listing your business on Google. Some of the benefits are obvious, but I'd like to give you an idea of the full picture and benefits you'll receive for listing your business. The best part of listing your business on Google is that it's free. You can use your house address (or even a friend's house) if you really wanted to. You just need to make sure you have access to the post-box to get the verification PIN that Google mails you.

Before we get into the steps of listing your marketing agency on Google My Business, let's talk about some things you need to do beforehand in order to adequately prepare for putting your business on the internet. The first thing you need is a valid telephone number. It's better to have a number with the same area code as your business address. That means you listing will rank better on Google search results if it's listed in New York and also has a New York number attached to the listing. If you verify your Google business listing in New York and use a California telephone number, Google won't give your listing as high of a priority in search rankings. With that being said, if you have a legal mailing address, a working telephone number and a website, you're ready to take advantage of the full benefits of adding your business to Google. Let's talk about the steps you'll use to register your business on Google search.

Step 1: Have your information ready and navigate to mybusiness.google.com

Step 2: Sign in with a Google account or the account you use for your Gmail. If you don't have a Google account, you can create one by clicking "start now", located on that same page.

Step 3: After you've signed in or registered your account, follow the on-screen prompts and enter your business info, including address, business name and phone number.

Step 4: Google will mail a postcard to your address within a few weeks. When you receive the postcard with a PIN, sign in to your account using the same method and enter your PIN.

Step 5: Your Google business page has been verified. You can sign in using the same method to optimize your listing, respond to reviews, add photos, write posts about promotions and much more.

Every business should be listed on Google. Google is the largest search engine in the world and Google listings are free, so you'd be silly not to take advantage of a Google listing. With more people launching online businesses, Google listings are also becoming more competitive. The sooner you register your Google My Business account and verify your business, the more relevant you'll appear to Google as you start getting more reviews. Google business listings also bring a significant amount of traffic to your site. My online marketing agency gets over 80% of its traffic from Google searches, many of which come from our Google listing. Although this chapter is focused on launching your Google business listing (also referred to as a business citation), it will help you to set up a listing on Yelp, Yellow Pages, Bing and other popular business search directories.

If you want a cheap and cost-effective way to get listed on hundreds of business directories, head over to http://www.fiverr.com. Fiverr is an online digital marketplace with most services priced at around $5. You'll find sellers there that will post your business on hundreds of sites for as little as that. Many of them use automated software to post business listings, which could potentially save you the several hours you'd spend doing it yourself.

If you've been following the steps I've laid out for you in this book, you should be proud of yourself. Most people who buy a book don't even get around to reading any of it. So far, we've been through actionable tips that you can use to launch and register your own online marketing agency, get your first few clients and scale your business. We just covered how to get found on major search directories and how to get a professional legal address for next to nothing. I'd like to spend the rest of this book teaching you the things I wish I knew when I started my own marketing agency. Now that you know the basics of how to get your business up and running, I want to teach you some tricks of the trade so that you have the confidence to go out there and apply the tips I'm teaching you. The next few chapters will focus on marketing your business and gaining more exposure. Then, we'll move onto clients and how to keep them happy and paying you. Launching a marketing agency is the easy part; the hardest part is learning how to keep people happy and how to work with lots of dynamic people at the same time. Every person is unique, so you'll need to learn a few interpersonal skills to minimize your stress level in business so that you can boost the morale of the people you're marketing for. You need to have a clear head to keep your clients confident and happy. If your clients lose their confidence in the work you're doing or even in their own businesses, they could stop paying you or worse – take their frustration out on you as well. Let's talk about some of the nuisances you'll encounter in this business and what you can do to stay on top of your game.

Phone Skills and Sales Call Techniques

You probably have a lot of questions about sales. How do you get new marketing agency clients? There are many ways you can get clients, but the number one strategy I recommend having is persistence. A consistent amount of persistence each day for months on end will always result in clients. It doesn't matter if you walk into 20 stores each day, or e-mail 50 people a day or post 10 Craigslist ads a day. If you do any of those things consistently enough and aren't afraid of rejection, you will get clients. The hard part is mustering up the energy and confidence to do it in the first place. It's even harder to have the resilience and thick skin to do it every single day of your life with little to no breaks.

The goal of asking people to purchase your services is to have them call you. If you can't immediately make the sale in person, then you want to get them on the phone with you and sell them remotely. This takes phone skills and confidence on the phone. Unfortunately, we live in an age where texting is favoured over telephone conversations and many people don't know how to use a phone with confidence. In this chapter, I want to teach you about some phone tips and sales call techniques that will help you close deals with new clients.

Like any skill, telephone confidence can't be taught overnight. You need to get comfortable using the phone and developing your phone personality so that it feels natural and comfortable to you. I was fortunate enough to grow up in a household where my parents constantly used the phone. At the age of four, I pretended to make my own cellphone out of cardboard and spoke on it for hours. At the age of 15, I called CBC Chief News Correspondent Peter Mansbridge and interviewed him on my radio show. In my second year of University, I spoke on the phone with the first Canadian to walk in space, Chris Hadfield. Up until this point, I've probably had thousands of hours of experience on the phone. This skill has allowed me to close a prospect on the phone at close to a 100% success rate. I always joke that if I went into sales with a large company that receives a lot of inbound leads that I'd be making way more that I would be at my own company. That may be true, but I can't imagine working for somebody else again now that I've tasted the freedom of working for myself.

I'm going to spend this chapter breaking down some phone skills that I've never heard anybody talk about before. Before I do, though, I'm going to cover the obvious stuff. In the future, I may write a book that focuses on telephone confidence and phone skills, but for now, I hope this chapter will suffice.

Here are the top phone skills I recommend you hone and practice:

Listen: It's important to listen and respond to what the people you're speaking to on the phone are saying. If you listen carefully, you can respond to your prospect's concerns and propose solutions that will make them feel comfortable hiring you.

Enunciate clearly: Speaking clearly and doing it naturally will give the person you're speaking with a sense of confidence in your professionalism and expertise. Just like dressing sharply to a job interview can boost your credibility as a candidate, enunciating while talking on the phone can make you seem more professional and intelligent.

Use inflection: Instead of speaking in a monotone voice during the entire conversation, use upwards inflections when you're speaking to get your prospects excited. The point of using inflection during a phone conversation is to appear more personable and human. It can also to generate positive emotions within the people you want to hire you.

Ask open-ended questions: Sometimes, asking open-ended questions can make your prospects feel listened to and appreciated. Instead of asking yes or no questions, ask your prospects about their struggles. "What were the biggest obstacles you faced this year in sales?" is a much better question that "Did you make a lot of sales?".

Use their name: Use the name of the person you're speaking to, and you'll build rapport quicker. People also pay closer attention to you when you use their name. It's a great way to get your prospect's full focus. You also seem more in control when you use peoples' names. You come across as more comfortable and commanding, but in a good way.

Now that we've covered some important phone skills, I want to give you one tip that will help boost your sales. Call your prospects and clients on the phone whenever possible. Call them before you've made the sale and after you have the client. By calling your clients, you remind them that you care about their business and that you're working for them. By calling your prospects before you've made a sale, you push them closer and closer to making a purchase.

If you have a client unsure about purchasing your service or product, call them and ask them why they haven't pulled the trigger yet. You cannot be persistent enough. The biggest problem salespeople face around the world is not using the phone enough. They barely do follow-up calls because they feel nervous about doing them. They feel like they don't want to bother their clients or prospects or that they've made enough sales this month to pay their bills and live comfortably. Avoiding calling a potential client is the biggest mistake you can ever make running your own business. When you run your own business, nobody is sitting there to employ you. If you don't make sales, your business will die.

Pick up the phone and call your prospects until they purchase your services. Think about it: have you ever been uncertain about a product, but bought it anyway because the salesperson was so persistent that you felt obligated to? If you've ever wondered why salespeople aren't loved by everyone, that's why. Salespeople are great at getting people to part with their money. You must get good at sales, too, if you want to run a successful marketing agency. When you grow, you can start hiring a sales team, but for now, you need to focus on making sales. Always remember that the phone is one of the most valuable weapons in your sales arsenal. If you're not using it every day, you're not using it enough.

Another important rule of making sales over the phone is to never wait for your prospects to contact you. If you've given a sales meeting or shown your product to a prospect and they said that they would get back to you, don't believe it. Prospects will rarely get back to you to give you their hard-earned money and purchase your services. Your best bet is to wait a few days (or until the specified a date they said they'll contact you has passed) and contact them first. A lot of people feel awkward about being persistent in sales and that's not for a bad reason. You may feel awkward about being persistent on the phone or anywhere you're making the sale is because you're sensing the tension within the prospective customer. That tension is real and it's because your potential client is forced to choose between saving their money and purchasing your services. You need to be their friend in this moment and tell them that making the purchase will make their life better. If you've followed my phone tips and built rapport with your customer, this should be a simple task for you.

So, what are you waiting for? Get out there and pick up the phone today. There's no time to waste. In the next chapter, we'll be talking about different ways to get inbound leads. If you don't know what inbound leads are, don't worry – we'll cover that and more!

How to Get Inbound Leads

Getting inbound leads is what's going to make your company sustainable. Every service-based industry needs to generate inbound leads if it wants to grow as fast as possible. Let's talk about leads and inbound leads so you understand what each of them are and how to generate them. The hardest leads to generate are inbound leads, so we'll focus on that in this chapter.

First of all, what is a lead? A lead is a prospective buyer who has not yet purchased your service or product. They know about your company and what you have to offer and it's your job to convert them into a buyer. There are three general stages that a lead will go through before they become a buyer. These are the awareness, consideration and decision stages. Below, I use the words prospect and lead interchangeably, so don't let that confuse you. A lead is technically a prospect, because they are in the process of becoming aware, considering and potentially deciding to purchase your product or service.

A prospect is somebody who is generally interested in your service.

Here are the three stages a lead will go through:

Awareness: This is the stage the prospect knows about your product or service and is expressing a problem that they need a solution to. In this stage, it's important not to try to sell your product immediately. You need to ask the right questions and make your client feel understood. This is the stage where you should be building rapport and confidence in your prospect.

Consideration: In this stage, you can inform your prospect about potential solutions, which can be a service or product that you provide. It's important not to sell your product in this stage. You need to behave like you believe the product will fit your client's needs. You need to still keep asking questions, so it noticeably appears that you're trying to probe your client to see if your product or service is a good match for them. After your lead becomes aware, it's your duty to make them consider your product or service.

Decision stage: This is the stage where your lead either makes the decision to go with your product or service or decides to go without it. This is where you should be confident and convince your prospect to make the decision to buy your product.

In the beginning stages of your business, you will generally have to go searching for your leads. This is often called prospecting or searching for outbound leads. Outbound leads are prospects you find yourself, whether that's through cold-calling businesses or walking onto business locations to sell your service face-to-face. This is one of the most time-consuming methods because it requires that you put in the initial energy to find clients. This is what you have to do in the beginning stages to get your business off the ground, but it isn't the best long-term strategy because it becomes draining and it's hard to scale unless you hire a team of trained salespeople to help you.

The best method you can use is a long-term strategy to acquire inbound leads. People who pick up the phone and call you first are the best customers out there. They're much easier to sell to because they already know about you and your product. Those people are often called "warm leads" and every business owner loves warm leads.

For example, Bell Mobility, one of the largest telephone service providers in Canada probably gets a lot of inbound warm leads because anybody who does a Google search of "cellphone providers in Canada" will come across their website and their services. They have door-to-door salespeople and online advertising too, but part of the reason they're so successful because their business is almost synonymous with telephone services in Canada, resulting in many people trying to sign up for their services before they even try to sell them. If you want to grow your marketing agency, you're going to have to implement similar tactics. You need to create a demand for your services and get seen on the internet if you want to generate inbound leads. In the next couple of pages, I'll talk about a few strategies you can use to generate inbound leads for your business.

Classified ads: Posting classified ads in the beginning stages of your business can result in thousands of dollars of sales a month. Check out websites like kijiji.com and craigslist.com and post at least 3 classified ads on each site a day for the entire week. Make posts about the services you provide and include eye-catching pictures in them. Write about the benefits you can achieve for their business and include your e-mail and phone number if you're comfortable with the latter. Before you know it, people will be calling and messaging you to inquire about your services. Remember the tip I taught you in the last chapter. Try to get them on the phone and build rapport with them. That will help you make the sale. Introduce a 12-month contract as soon as you can, and you may have that client paying you for the entire year.

Facebook ads: This book isn't a Facebook ads course. Facebook ads are quite technical, but anybody can learn how to launch them on the cheap. Check out YouTube And Udemy for lessons on how to launch Facebook ads for leads to your website.

Content marketing: Create social media accounts for your marketing agency. Aim to have a YouTube, Twitter, Instagram and Facebook account for your agency and release relevant content on it every day. Give free value such as marketing tips and tricks and do everything you can to grow your accounts. In the long run, this will bring you more visitors. After a couple years of doing this, you can attract dozens of daily prospects. Remember, content marketing takes time. The longer and more consistently you do it for, the better results you will get.

Blog posts: Writing blog posts on your website or on www.medium.com will help you generate leads. If you write a viral blog post, your business can explode overnight. Write consistently and try to have a weekly goal for how many blog posts you're going to write and how many words they're going to be. Remember, the goal isn't to expect instant results – it's to put consistent value into the world for a long period of time so that you build credibility. Don't get frustrated after a few months of creating content and writing blog posts because they aren't generating leads. Over time, linking back to your website and publishing posts on your website will boost your Google SEO ranking and make your website rank higher on search results.

Don't forget that inbound leads take time and shouldn't be a short-term goal. There's a lot of competition on the internet and many people who are vying to grow their own online marketing agencies. You're going to have to give more upfront value at a more consistent rate if you want to be successful. Nobody said this business was going to be easy, but if you keep trying, you will ultimately succeed in the digital marketing space.

How to Deal with Problems and Conflicts

We've covered the basics of starting and successfully running your own marketing agency. We've also talked about different ways you can market your business, improve your phone and sales skills and get new clients. Now it's time to talk about some of the problems you may run into running your marketing agency. Everybody runs into problems and conflicts in business and in life. You'll face situations where you don't get along with clients no matter what. It's virtually unavoidable if you want to do business on a large scale. A big part of being an entrepreneur is putting out fires and keeping everyone happy. Keeping your business under control is what I'll teach you how to do in this chapter, all while remaining calm.

So, what do you do when you run into a problem with a client? My best piece of advice for you is to hang on. What I mean by that is to keep as many clients as you can, even if they're on your case or are a slight inconvenience. Listen to their problems and concerns and try to fix them instead of giving them a refund. You need to develop an attitude where you can stomach adversity and not let affect you. If you manage to do this, you will beat your competition by a long shot. Remind yourself that there's no reason to get stressed and that a client cannot do any damage to you or your business. You work in the marketing industry. Even if a client were to slander your business unfairly, you would find a way to correct it because you're a digital marketing legend.

When you're dealing with problems in business, the best thing to do is to calm your client down. Listen to their concerns, apologize if necessary and fix the problem. Don't be afraid to put your foot down. Being a pushover won't help you in the long-run because your clients will think you're a pushover. When people think you're a pushover, they try to get free things from you and squeeze you like a lemon. Find a happy medium where you can listen to your client's concerns and fix them while remaining civil.

I often get questions about refunds. What should you do when a client asks for a refund? The answer to this is that it's up to you. If you've completed a month of work for the client and sunk your time and energy into it, don't refund them. Have a no refund policy once the contract is up. If you've worked 15 out of the 30-day contract period, you may choose to refund your client half of the contract price. It is always up to you, but it's important to mention these terms beforehand in writing for added protection. If you want to avoid mentioning this in writing every time, have a refund policy on your website or add it to your contract template. Check the consumer protection laws in your business location to make sure you're doing everything legally and ethically.

The bottom line is, you want to retain as many clients and as much money as possible. You should set your terms beforehand so doing this is easy. Always provide the best quality work and track the work you've been doing throughout the entire process, so you can justify not having to give disgruntled clients a full refund every time. Let's be honest here, you're a small-business owner that provides services. You're not selling gardening equipment that you can simply refund. The time you sink into projects is valuable time you'll never get back ever again. That's why my refund policy is much tighter than somebody's refund policy might be in a product-based industry. When somebody gets a refund, I don't get my time and energy back like I would if they were refunding a product. Always keep this in mind and don't be shy to tell your clients this if you happen to get into a disagreement.

Sometimes, at your own discretion, it may benefit you and the client to provide some extra work if they're dissatisfied with what you've done. This isn't always the best case, however. You want to make sure the people you're working with aren't taking advantage of you and your valuable time you could spend prospecting and helping your other clients. If you think your client has a point and you could have done better or fell short of your promises, then of course give them extra time or added services for a limited time. However, you don't have to reward rude behaviour if it isn't justified.

Create legal contracts that outline your contract terms and deliverables. This will protect you in the long run. My recommendations in the chapter about creating legal contracts will help you out. Also remember to check out my Udemy course, which provides information about dealing with clients in every stage of your business. Problems are simply part of running a business – there's no avoiding it. Your goal is to minimize the amount of problems and have the protection required to deal with them in the event that they pop up.

In the next chapter, we'll talk about insurance for your marketing agency for when you start making more money and getting new clients for your digital marketing agency. Insurance isn't a mandatory part of launching your own marketing agency, but it's something you can consider if you want peace of mind. This is less of a concrete tip, but if you're stressed out about your business, it may also be time to hire a personal assistant or a virtual assistant (VA). We'll also talk about that in the chapters ahead.

Errors and Omissions Insurance

Errors and omissions insurance are a form of professional liability insurance, meaning it offers protection from malpractice. This is also commonly referred to as E&O insurance. If you're wondering whether you need E&O insurance, ask yourself this question: can I make a mistake in my business that will cause somebody else to sue me?" The answer in digital marketing is yes. It may not be as serious as making an error as a brain surgeon, but it's definitely something to consider as your business grows and you start working with larger companies that are being scrutinized by millions of people and the media.

I'm not going to elaborate too much on E&O insurance because most marketing agencies choose to forgo it, especially in the beginning stages. If you're not making much money yet (just enough to pay your bills and make profit), you shouldn't be looking into buying insurance. Insurance is a repeated expense you should avoid in the early beginning stages of starting your marketing agency. If you're working with smaller contracts or local clients who want you to do simple marketing tasks, professional liability insurance will only burn a hole in your wallet. It's something you should look at when you start making enough revenue and want to protect your assets.

One of the best advantages of purchasing insurance when you're ready is peace of mind. Knowing you're protected is a great feeling and will give you the confidence to make decisions and not have to worry about somebody suing you. When it comes down to how much insurance you should buy, I recommend asking fellow business owners or speaking with a broker who can help you. Now that you know how sales work, find a trustworthy broker who listens to your needs and concerns.

A cheaper and more cost-effective way of dealing with issues and getting more work done is to hire a virtual assistant in a less economically-developed nation. That way, you can have somebody wake you up in the morning, respond to client inquiries, update you about issues of importance and much more. Hiring an online virtual assistant can also make being an entrepreneur less lonely.

Hiring a Virtual Assistant

Growing a company can be difficult and time consuming. That's why it's important to automate your business to a certain extent and delegate some of the less important tasks. Instead of spending hours answering e-mails and filling out spreadsheets, you could be focusing on tasks that bring you more profit and grow your business. Since cash is the lifeblood of your business, you want to be able to make as much of it as possible for steady and consistent growth. No amount of income is worth burning out and not enjoying your life. In this chapter, I'll teach you everything about hiring a virtual assistant from learning about what tasks to delegate, to hiring a fairly-priced assistant.

If you're struggling to get all your tasks completed daily, but you're still generating a steady positive income, you should consider hiring a virtual assistant, especially if you're a sole proprietor or a one-person show. You need to get used to giving tasks to your team. The purpose of a virtual assistant (VA) is to take the work off your back and allow you to generate more income. It's a much cheaper solution when you're starting out than hiring a full-time or part-time employee at your physical location.

By outsourcing some of the work to an assistant in another country, you can save hundreds or even thousands of dollars in the long run. They can help you at a surprisingly low cost and reduce the amount of time you need to work on your business. By hiring a good VA, you'll be better rested, learn how to teach others to manage your business for you and even put some of your income on autopilot. The best part is that your VA can work while you sleep, so you'll wake up to an inbox full of completed tasks – or even an empty inbox because your VA took care of all your e-mails!

What Can VAs Do for My Business?

The possibilities are infinite, but here are just a few things your VA can do for you and your business:

1. Handle and respond to e-mails.
2. Write blog posts.
3. Wake you up in the morning.
4. Order groceries and supplies.
5. Do simple research.
6. Update your clients.
7. Create and fill out spreadsheets.
8. Post classified ads.
9. Write notes.

It doesn't stop there! If you can think it, you can probably find a VA who can do it. If you're wondering where to hire a VA, just do a simple Google search or use a freelancer platform like Fiverr, Upwork, Freelancer, or any other online marketplace. Some popular agencies where you can hire virtual assistance are Tasks Everyday, Your Man in India, Get Friday and much more. A simple search of any of those terms will bring up the websites. If you go with a company instead of an individual Freelancer, then you'll get more protection in case your VA gets sick or has an accident. Agencies can replace your VAs immediately, but they are usually the more expensive option. Many of them do accept phone calls 24/7, which gives business owners reliability.

How Much Should You Pay for a VA?

There is no simple answer to this question because there are many factors that influence cost, but we'll narrow it down for you. If you hire a VA from India or Nepal, you can expect to pay anything from $50 - 150 a month for 10-15 tasks a month. You can drive this cost lower if you seek an individual Freelancer form one of the sites we recommended above.

Speak with them individually and let them barter against themselves. Either offer a really low rate and meet somewhere in the middle or ask them if they can go any lower. When you phrase it that way, they will usually lower their rates. If they don't, then rinse and repeat until you find a VA that beliefs in your principles, business ideas and budget. When it comes to the cost of a VA, you should consider the number of tasks you'll have them do each month, the size of your business and the complexity of the tasks you're delegating.

When It Pays to Have a VA

It helps to have a VA under any circumstances, but you'll really notice how helpful they are when:

1. You get thousands of e-mails a day and they manage them for you.
2. You're travelling, and they take care of your customers.
3. They start understanding your business goals and make thoughtful suggestions.

They schedule content to publish on social media for inbound marketing purposes. They start making small decisions for your business, so you don't have to. They do the time-consuming work that's less profitable like filling out spreadsheets. If you're working longer hours than you want or doing tasks that you can't stand, then you should consider looking for a VA to take some of the work off your shoulders.

Your Agency's Next Steps

Once you start getting more business and increasing your revenue, you need to put your business before yourself. What I mean by this is that you need to stop spending all your money unnecessarily, and instead start putting your income back into your business. Go to your local bank and open a business account. Make sure that when your clients pay you, your income goes directly in there. You need to start paying yourself 10% or less from those earnings. If that doesn't leave you with enough money, that's good. That means you need to start selling more an expanding your business.

I know I told you to start off as a sole proprietor and accept the simplest business model, but if you really want to scale your company and take control of your financial destiny, you need to make your company its own entity. Incorporate your business or form an LLC to offer you protection. This will separate your personal assets from your business assets and will ensure your business still exists after you do. If you want to be in the top 5% of all digital agencies out there, you need to think of your marketing agency as its own person.

You need to be far-sighted from now on. Get more retainers to pay you monthly, because that will be the lifeblood of your business and allow you to grow your company. Your mind shouldn't be focused on how to get that new car or buy that new house. You need to focus on how you can provide the most value to the most people. I tripled my income when I started thinking about the client first. I made online courses, signed more clients and here I am, arming you with the knowledge and power to go do the same thing I did. In fact, I encourage you to do better and dream of doing even more. Use the next six months to learn as much as you can about digital marketing and to stay on top of your industry. There's so much great content in books and on the internet that will teach you so much more about digital marketing today. You'll also learn a lot through trial and error in the coming years. Don't be afraid to try new things or to take on big clients.

Believe in yourself and that you'll see every project and task through until the end and you will do it.

I'm so proud of you for taking your first steps towards launching your own digital marketing agency. Starting a business is no easy feat, and running one that you can grow for an extended period of time is even harder. I know that no matter what, you'll achieve great things and be able to work for yourself for a long time to come. If you have any questions, feel free to e-mail me, because I'd love to hear from you and help you out in any way I can. You can also enroll in my Udemy course free of charge and ask a question in the Q&A section. That will allow me to create a video response for you so that you can follow along on your computer, tablet or mobile device.

I wish you and your agency all the best in the future. Remember that a digital marketing business is something that takes a lot of consistency to grow. Most of your clients will not come organically. You're going to need to push as hard as you can in the beginning stages to create a snowball effect. Use your new business as an opportunity to meet great people, improve your life and learn about what people do for a living. This business will teach you a lot about the business models of other people, which is invaluable. Few careers expose you to so many different people and businesses as intimately as digital marketing does. You are the backbone of people's livelihood, because you generate the attention they need to make a profit and be successful. I wish you the best of luck.

About the Author

As a marketing director and former multimedia producer, I have been noted for my creative vision, innovative sense of direction and happy work ethic. I have over seven years of experience in the media industry, creating content on a national and international scale for businesses and media networks. I have experience in radio broadcast, social media marketing, PR and publishing. I have additional experience with political interviews, news reporting, audio production and voiceovers. I have collaborated and cross-promoted with individuals in the entertainment industry for three years, including artists featured by Universal Motown, Vevo, CBC and more. I have experienced media in the public eye and behind the scenes, giving me the ability to tackle multifaceted undertakings with efficiency and ease.

My productions have been featured on CBC, Fullscreen, CHEX Television, Disney's Maker Gen Studios and more. I have hosted radio interviews with CBC Chief News Correspondent Peter Mansbridge, Canadian Astronaut Chris Hadfield and host of the Next Chapter, Shelagh Rogers. I also had the opportunity to produce videos alongside Canadian author Sigmund Brouwer as a video producer for Rock and Roll Literacy.

I work full-time at my marketing agency. I provide start-up development, reputation and trust management, social media marketing, and media relations services to clients across the globe. I teach the number one course on the internet for removing negative Google links and have worked with Fortune 1000 companies to mitigate damage to their reputation and boost their influence in the media.

In my spare time, I teach online courses and have approximately 15,000 students from over 160 countries taking my courses on marketing, self-development, audio production and public speaking. To find out more about me, please visit my personal site at **www.nadernejad.com**.

What are my students saying about the online course?

"This course is gold! I love it"

- **Samuel Oluwakayode**

"Solid course. I've worked in freelance digital marketing and this is exactly what I need to turn my side-hustle into a business. You're really good at pumping up your audience. I'm only a few lectures in and I know how to set up my website and the business model. Thanks Nader!"

- **Dalton Miles**

"Very, very practical advice. I wish I had this video when I first started. I'm reviewing Nader's videos to get a refresher to see if I'm missing any ideas. I liked the pricing package section since it helped me realize that I'm selling myself short in some of my packages. I would recommend this for anyone starting any business."

- **Milton Wani**

If you are unable to enroll in the course for any reason, please contact me directly at my e-mail address, **nader@nadernejad.com**

www.ingramcontent.com/pod-product-compliance
Lightning Source LLC
Chambersburg PA
CBHW031928240526
45464CB00023B/2339